YOUR KNOWLEDGE HAS VALUE

AF144743

- We will publish your bachelor's and master's thesis, essays and papers

- Your own eBook and book - sold worldwide in all relevant shops

- Earn money with each sale

Upload your text at www.GRIN.com
and publish for free

The Conflict between Herders and Farmers in the Middle-Belt Nigeria

Alloy Ihuah

Bibliographic information published by the German National Library:

The German National Library lists this publication in the National Bibliography; detailed bibliographic data are available on the Internet at http://dnb.dnb.de.

ISBN: 9783346589354
This book is also available as an ebook.

© GRIN Publishing GmbH
Nymphenburger Straße 86
80636 München

Print and binding: Books on Demand GmbH, Norderstedt, Germany
Printed on acid-free paper from responsible sources.

The present work has been carefully prepared. Nevertheless, authors and publishers do not incur liability for the correctness of information, notes, links and advice as well as any printing errors.

GRIN web shop: https://www.grin.com/document/1148812

HERDERS AND FARMERS CONFLICTS IN THE MIDDLE-BELT NIGERIA:
TOWARDS A PHILOSOPHY OF HUMAN INTEGRATION.

BY

Alloy S. Ihuah, PhD[1]

Table of content

Introduction 2

The Problem of Ethnic Agitations and Ethnic Cleansing in Nigeria 3

Causes of Ethno-Religious Conflicts in Nigeria 6

Understanding Interfaith Concept and its Actors in Nigeria 9

Enhancement of a Philosophy of Human Integration in Nigeria. 12

Conclusion 15

---

[1] Alloy S. Ihuah, PhD, is Professor of Philosophy, Benue State University, Makurdi- Nigeria.

Introduction

The history of ethnicity and ethnic conflicts in Nigeria is also traced back to the colonial transgressions that forced the ethnic groups of the northern and southern provinces to become an entity called Nigeria in 1914. This generated hatred and conflict among different ethnic groups. The task of addressing this seed of conflict planted by the British has been a complex one.[2] These conflicts as it were and as it is, possesses within themselves the tendency of hampering the peace and collective existence of Nigeria if not checked and curtail. This notwithstanding, a stable, secured, and peaceful relations amongst the diverse and heterogeneous ethnic groups in a Nigeria for development and sustainable development is both timely and imperative. In such a time in the history of the nation as this, when the nation is confronted and affronted with numerous challenges of national development that have to a large extent threatened our collective existence, the need to de-emphasis those things the divides us and to emphasis those things that unites becomes more glaring and crystal clear. This thinking is based on the fact that without a peaceful relation between the diverse ethnic groups in Nigeria, there can be no secured and stable Nigeria and without a stable and secured Nigeria, the much-needed development and the change that have been clamored for by Nigerians will amount to a mirage.

This paper advances a scan of interfaith concept as an enduring harmony among the divergent ethnic groups in Nigeria. In doing this, the paper takes cognizance the problem of ethnic agitations and conflicts in Nigeria, the causes of ethnic and religious crisis in Nigeria, an understanding of interfaith concept and its actors in Nigeria, and advances arguments for the fact that the inadequacies of interfaith concept notwithstanding, it is an enduring philosophy that can be activated by Nigeria for the enhancement of stable, secured and peaceful relations amongst the diverse ethnic nationalities in Nigeria. In the final third, this paper advances a philosophy of ethnic and religious tolerance in view of the fact that despite the diversity in tribes and faith, we share the same humanity and that it is only on the basis of this tolerance and the mutual respect for one another's faith that the peace and unity that is both necessary and imperative for national development and nation building can be attained.

---

[2] Ray Ikechukwu Jacob "A Historical Survey of Ethnic Conflict in Nigeria" in the *Asian Social Science* Vol. 8, No. 4; April 2012.

The Problem of Ethnic Agitations and Ethnic Cleansing in Nigeria

A cursory look as the Nigerian existential situation reveals the problem of ethnic agitations. In Nigeria today virtually all the various ethnic groups talk about marginalization and domination, hence all the ethnic groups are affected one way or the other by the national question. Momoh illustrates this thus:

> For the Niger-Delta and oil producing minority it is exploitation and environmental degradation; for the Igbo it is marginalization; for the Hausa Fulani, it is uneven development; for the minorities of the North, particularly the Middle Belt it is one of internal colonialism; for the Yoruba it is power exclusion. Hence everybody is demanding empowerment on the basis of one assumption – xenophobia[3].

The perceived marginalization constitutes the building blocks for the numerous crisis and upheavals in the history of the Nigerian state. Discourse on the subject matter of conflict (ethnic or religious), with particular reference to Nigeria have attained philosophical maturity and hence, there has been a massive policy attention in this regard. This is partly due to the repeated instances of collective violence: while analysts differ in their assessment, most agree that the early 1980s and the transition to democracy in 1999 both witnessed an upsurge in communal and ethnic conflicts and violence in Nigeria. For example, in mapping violence across Nigeria, Elaigwu[4] estimates that between 1980 and 2005 there were at least 140 violent inter-group conflicts in Nigeria, resulting in the loss of lives and property. Alubo states that "over 80 major eruptions of violence took place between May 1999 and December 2003 in Nigeria, which, he notes, was three-fold the number that occurred during the eight-year rule of General Babangida regime between 1985 and 1993... 300,000 deaths during the period would not be an over estimate"[5]. It is in the same thinking that Kirk-Greene posits that "since 1914 the Nigerian socio-political scene has been bedeviled by sets of opposing factors each widening the wound and reducing the hope of healing it: North vs. South; Islam vs. Christianity; alleged feudalism vs. achieved elitism; haves vs. have-nots, each with sinister undertones, tensions, irreconcilability and threatened withdrawal. These obvious or tacit dichotomous elements had always been used

---

[3] Quoted In Johnson Olusegun Ajayi "Resurgence of Ethnic Crises and Instability in Nigeria" in Research on Humanities and Social Sciences. Vol.4, No.21, 2014. P. 51.
[4] Quoted in Islamic actors and Interfaith Relations in Northern Nigeria Policy Paper No1, March 2013. P. 16
[5] Ibid.

by the so-called Nigerian nationalists to further the forces of disunity and fire the embers of tension and interethnic hatred which often climaxed in persistent violent crises"[6].

Many of these disturbances had ethnic as well as religious connotations; moreover, they have occurred within as well as between Muslim and Christian communities. In general terms, it has been argued that ethnicity's significance as a marker of difference and an identifier for potential targets of violence slowly gave way to the salience of religion. As a consequence, religion is often quoted as one of the factors influencing processes of violent escalation; at the same time, collective violence is hardly ever exclusively, or even predominantly, 'religious' in nature. 'Christian' and 'Muslim' conflicting actors are often also divided along ethnic, regional, or party-political lines, which blurs the defining role of religion in these situations.

If we look more closely at the religious actors involved in violent conflict, it should be noted that inter-religious conflict between Christians and Muslims is now more prevalent than intra-Islamic conflict between different groups, especially from the middle of the 1970s – with the obvious exception, of course, of the struggles around Boko Haram. The intra-Muslim dimensions of violence are often ignored because of the more sensation Muslim-Christian violence. More recently, in Bukuru in Plateau State, and in Gonin-Gora on the outskirts of Kaduna, allegations of Christian violence targeting unsuspecting Muslims has been raised.

Several cases stand out as 'key instances' of collective violence. Prime examples are perhaps the *Maitatsine* riots in Kano, Maiduguri and other parts of the north in the 1980s, and the violence in Kafanchan in 1987; the latter marked the starting of the shift from ethnic or intra-Muslim conflicts that were predominant from the 1950s until the 1980s, to Christian- Muslim confrontations that have been dominant since the late 1980s. Other prominent 'key instances' of violent conflict include the Christian-Muslim violence in Zangon Kataf LGA in Kaduna State in 1992; the 1999/2000 Kaduna violence following the re-introduction of *sharia;* the 2004 violence in Plateau and Kano States; and several other cases in Plateau State[7]. Others are the Jukun-Tiv

---

[6] Johnson Ajayi "Resurgence of Ethnic Crises and Instability in Nigeria" in *Research on Humanities and Social Sciences* Vol.4, No.21, 2014. P. 50.
[7] Islamic actors and Interfaith Relations in Northern Nigeria Policy Paper No1, March 2013. P 17.

conflicts in Wukari, in the Fulani-Sayawa conflicts in Tafawa Balewa, and in the Igbo-Ora interventions in Oyo state.

Time and space do not permit a detail historical analysis of ethnic and communal conflict and violence in Nigeria but what is to be noted is that at every historical junction where these crisis and conflicts raises their ugly heads in Nigeria, efforts are made to stem their tide through the setting up of commission of inquiries into the remote and immediate causes of same. Be that as it may, these crisis and conflicts keep reoccurring. While it is accepted as true, the fact that in human existential life, crisis is bound to occur, Ajayi[8] chronicles the following factors can be said to account for the continual reoccurrence of these ethno-religious crisis:

i. horizontal (intergroup) economic, political, and cultural inequalities;

ii. the salience, overlaps, and intersections between ethnic, religious, and regional boundaries;

iii. the negative effects of the political institutions of 'indigeneity';

iv. the historical legacy of indirect rule;

v. the politicization of religious and ethnic identities and the resulting political competition, especially in situations of political change (e.g. redrawing political boundaries) and instability;

vi. the inability of the state to stem the negative effects of protracted economic crisis, to ensure public order, and to implement post-conflict peace building measures;

vii. the 'youth bulge', combined with exploding youth unemployment rates and the corresponding 'availability' of some young men to engage in illicit behaviour, including political violence; this is particularly significant when politicians hire these youths to cause havoc, a practice that many consider common occurrence;

viii. the heavy-handedness of Nigeria's security forces in resolving situations of violent escalation, or even their active involvement in aggravating such tense situations; and

ix. Other, more generic factors, such as group size and resource competition (e.g. over oil revenues and land).

---

[8] Johnson Ajayi, *Resurgence of Ethnic Crises and Instability in Nigeria*, p18.

Causes of Ethno-Religious Conflicts in Nigeria

Ethnicity is natural in almost all societies made up of numerous ethnic groups. Scholars have identified several causal factors responsible for conflicts and crisis in Nigerian, a rehearsal of a few of them is here considered necessary. The very first of such causes and most important of all in the opinion of this paper is corruption. Nwankwo corroborated the above when he asserted that "corruption is considered to be one of the main causes of ethno-religious conflicts"[9]. A high level of corruption and the looting of state resources is another serious and 'pandemic' problem that makes all forms of conflict and trouble worse in Nigeria. The country is 'richly endowed with natural resources and high-quality human capital', but corruption is one of the main reasons that affect the development of the country in a negative way. The appropriation of state resources by certain hands makes poverty and bitter anger inevitable aspects of daily socio-economic and political routine. In this sense, though corruption is not peculiar to Nigeria, many sources call it the 'bane of the country'. Poverty and injustice caused by corruption weaken any sense of mutual tolerance, social solidarity or coexistence, while reawakening social hatred, radicalism and violence. For this reason, corruption is seen as one of the most important issues that must be resolved in order to cope with ethno-religious conflicts in Nigeria[10].

In fact, the 'failure' of the Nigerian political elite to enact good laws, promote national integration and foster good economic progress via thoughtful and pronounced policies has resulted in massive unemployment. This has in turn led to the rise of communal, ethnic and religious conflicts that are characteristic of the Nigerian politics. Since poverty and unemployment have acted as the mainstay for various ethno-religious conflicts in the country, an accumulation of pauperised people can end up acting as paid militants. This could be the reason why any conflict in Nigeria is usually characterized by many fighters[11].

---

[9] Nwankwo, quoted in Haldun Canci and Adedoyin Odukoya "Ethnic and Religious Crisis in Nigeria: A Specific Analysis Upon Identities (1999-2013)" in the *African Journal of Crisis Resolution 2016. Vol. 1.* P. 2.
[10] Haldun Canci and Adedoyin Odukoya "Ethnic and Religious Crisis in Nigeria: A Specific Analysis Upon Identities (1999-2013)" in the *African Journal of Crisis Resolution 2016. Vol. 1.* P. 2.
[11] See Mu'asu, Abubakar 2011. Understanding the emerging trends of terrorism in Nigeria: A case study of Boko Haram and similar groups. *Responding to emerging trends of terrorism in Nigeria.* Conference proceedings, monograph series 16. Lagos, CLEEN Foundation. pp. 10-21. Available from:

Another casual factor fueling ethno-religious crisis in Nigeria is that as relating to a perceived ethnic and religious discrimination. At different levels and times in the past, "the Nigerian people have complained of religious and ethnic discrimination. Most ask for religious and ethnic rights within their state. Another cause of the conflicts has been the state's use of religion and ethnicity in political discourse or action. Therefore, it is clear that accusations and allegations of neglect, oppression and domination are the major causes that fuel ethno-religious conflicts[12]. It is in this sense that it has been argued that "ethnic conflict is a sign of a weak state, or a state embroiled in ancient loyalties. In this case, states act with bias to favor a particular ethnic group or region, and behaviors such as preferential treatment fuel ethnic conflicts[13].

Another factor that provokes conflict in the Nigeria is that the culprits that mastermind these dastardly and abominable acts in the regions go unpunished and escape unhurt. Successive administration, like military and civilian, since independence has always paid lip service and deaf ear to bringing the perpetrators to book. Moreover, numerous religious uprisings, especially in the northern part of the country with its attendant consequences in the socio-economic and political development in the country has been appealing to the leaders of the country. This is premised on the fact that Nigeria has been ruled majorly by the north and the emerging leaders see the situation as a means of bridging the development gap between them and the more prosperous south. Emphasis is not lacking as there was no political will on the part of the leadership to bring to book the perpetrators of the Maitasine riots of the 1980s; Kano Riots of 1991, Sharia Riots of 2000, the Jos Mayhem of 2004 and 2010 respectively. As a result of government's insensitivity of the problem under reference, the culprits that were arrested were later released in the law court for lack of evidence[14]. Following closely on the problem of leaving the perpetrators of violence to go unpunished and the weak institutional mechanisms to check these abuses was apathy and failure of security and intelligence agencies to live up to expectation in confronting the challenge. The case in point here is the open declaration of war on the Nigerian state by the leadership of Miyetti Allah Kautal Hore without their apprehension and arrest by the security agencies. The said Fulani socio-cultural organization had promised to

http://www.cleen.org/Responding%20to%20the%20Emergining%20Trends%20of%20Terrorism%20in%20Nigeria.pdf> [Accessed 25 July 2018].
[12] Op. Cit. P. 3
[13] Ray Ikechukwu Joseph P. 22
[14] Ibid P. 22.

mobilize all Fulani in the West African sub region to converge in Benue and by implication, the Nigerian state, to kill and maim its inhabitants[15]. Notwithstanding these treasonable and inciting utterances by Miyetti Allah, its leadership has not been arrested, tried and made to account for their actions against the Nigerian State. What this clearly shows is that those fomenting crisis, including the bloody clashes in Benue, Taraba, Zamfara, Nassarawa, Plateau, Kaduna, Edo, Borno, Yobe, Enugu, Kogi, Adamawa and other parts of Nigeria, have political backers, who now want to channel them to achieve their unpatriotic quest to subvert our constitution and forcefully take over the National Government.

Lastly, conflict of interest between the diverse ethnic groups have also accounted for the recurrent ethnic and ethno-religious crisis in Nigeria, Haldun Canci and Adedoyin Odukoya succinctly corroborated the above in the following lines:

> Nigeria, like many other countries in the world, lacks a consensus on how necessary changes and reforms are effected. This is caused by the fact that different religious and ethnic groups have varying benefits in which case some groups will have their interests met while others will not. This means that tension occurs when individuals who feel that they are deprived attempt to increase their stake of power or wealth or to alter the central beliefs, values, norms and philosophies.[16]

Ethnic and religious skirmishes and conflicts have resulted in political instability. As a phenomenon, political instability has itself connoted several implications for the country. For instances, there has been a state of unconducive atmosphere for taking and effecting viable decisions making and actions by the leaders. Under a condition of instability, the people and the leadership are distracted by pursuing their self-fish ambitions and embezzlement of national cake and resources. Again, the existence of political instability arising from ethnic inclination and marginalization has been discontinuity in policies and programmes. The series of policy discontinuity registered in the country have successfully undermined the attainment of socio-economic advancement for the country. Analysts, generally, agree on the relevance of policy

---

[15] Saturday Sun Newspaper, 13/01/2018
[16] Op. Cit. Haldun Canci and Adedoyin Odukoya, P. 3.

continually for the attainment of socio-economic development[17]. It is in this regards that the question of what should be the cultural philosophy and underlining principle that can drive a programme of action as well as lead to the enhancement of a stable, secured and a peace relation amongst the diverse ethnic nationalities in Nigeria comes to mind.

Understanding Interfaith Concept and its Actors in Nigeria

According to Wesley Ariarajah, inter-faith dialogue is seen as a "way not only to become informed about the faiths of others but also to rediscover essential dimensions of one's own faith tradition. The benefits of removing historical prejudices and enmities as well as new possibilities for working together for common good are recognized and affirmed"[18]. In this context, interfaith concept can be defined as "an ecumenical attempt to bring people of different faith together on the platform of peaceful co-existence, co-operation and tolerance"[19]. In the HarperCollins Dictionary of Religion, it is presented as "a process of interreligious understanding that demands mutual respect and the requirement that a description of another's religion be affirmed by the member of that religion"[20]. Another definition would be that dialogues "held among religions, involve discussions on religious beliefs and their practices which is the framework in every discussion, as well as those connected with issues of culture and ethnic or the race of various religions"[21].

---

[17] Op. Cit. Ray, Ikechukwu Jacob. P. 24.
[18] Wesley Ariarajah, "Interfaith Dialogue" in *Dictionary of the Ecumenical Movement* 2nd Edition, edited by Nicholas Lossky et al. (Geneva, WCC Publications 2002) P. 314.
[19] Daniji, F. *Conflict Resolution Studies in Africa* (Nigeria: Meks Links Publisher, 2007). P. 31.
[20] Jonathan Z. Smith. *The Harpercollins Dictionary of Religion*. (London: Harper Collins Publishers, 1996), 317.
[21] John M. Sutcliffe. *A Dictionary of Religious Education*. (London: SCM Press Ltd, 1984), P. 112

Relations between Christianity and Islam over a period of fourteen centuries have ranged from conflict to concord, from polemics to dialogue, from commercial cooperation to open confrontation. Christian-Muslim relations however they manifest, constitute an important global phenomenon and affect the future of vast multitudes of people. With Christians and Muslims accounting for sixty percent of the world's population, relations between the two religions demand serious study and engagement. Over the past half century, Christian-Muslim dialogue has become especially popular. Conferences, meetings, oral and written exchanges and round-table discussions have taken place in nearly every corner of the globe. Yet most of these discussions are more monologues than dialogues. They usually represent a predominantly Western perspective and often are unapologetically liberal in their outlook and their idealist models of how Christian-Muslim relations ought to be. In addition, they smack of Western guilt and remorse for past failures and shortcomings. This paper strongly affirms the importance of moving beyond what Lamin Sanneh has described as "a paralyzing guilt complex"[22] to fully grapple with the real-life experiences of Christians and Muslims in different cultural contexts.

The major actors in the interfaith relation in Nigeria are the adherents of Christianity and Islam-the Christians and Muslims. This elevation is based on the fact that these religions constitute the major religions in the nation. An exposition of the kind of relations that have been advocated for by these religious traditions is here considered necessary in other to arrive at the imperative of interfaith concept or dialogue in the task of enhancing a stable and a peaceful Nigeria.

Scriptural and historical records revealed the early cordial interactions between Muslims and Christians. This was practically demonstrated by the Abyssinian Christians through the good leadership and non-discriminatory qualities of Negus who gave warm reception to the Muslim refugees persecuted in Makkah[23]. The Holy Qur'an describes the early Christians as friends of Muslims thus:

---

[22] Lamin Sanneh, Peity and Power: Muslims and Christians in West Africa (New York: Orbis Books, 1996), p. 5.
[23] Hitti, P.K. *History of the Arabs.* (London: McMillan Publisher, 1970) Quoted in Toki, T.O et'al "Peace building and Interfaith Dialogue in Nigeria" in the *Journal of Islam in Nigeria*. Vol 1 No. 1, June, 2015. P. 105

> You will find that the people most violently hostile towards those who believe are the Jews and those who associate (others with God): while you will find the most affectionate among them towards those who believe are those who say; we are Christian. That is because some of them are priests and monks, they do not behave proudly[24].

Deducible from the above is the fact that the most holy Qu'ran elevated and emphasized a brotherly relationship regardless of geographical affinity or religions. "Under the Abbasid government, the Muslim interacted with the Jews and Christians on ideal basis through the accommodation of rights to freedom of religion and security of life. They had right to practice their religion in synagogues and Monasteries in Baghdad"[25]. The holy Qur'an unequivocally supports a hitch-free interfaith and inter-religious dialogue and relations in the following verses: "Say O people of the Book! Come to common terms as between us and you: that we worship none but Allah: that we associate no partners with Him that we erect not, from among ourselves lords and patrons other than Allah"[26]. Dialogue must take place in a conducive atmosphere of trust and readiness for harmony. Islam encourages dialogue as a peace building approach capable of resolving differences and disagreement between followers of divergent faiths[27]. However, this must be in line with the Islamic regulative guidelines as contained in the Qur'an: "Invite all to the way of your Lord with wisdom and beautiful preaching and argue with them in the ways that are best[28].

Many biblical passages also encourage good neighborliness devoid of hostility with non-Christians as elucidated in John 14:16, Matt: 5:17 and Matt: 22:40. In 1st Thessalonians 5:21, the Bible gives methodological guideline on Dialogue: "Prove all things and hold fast to that which is the truth"[29] Islam entrusts the safety of one another on his fellow human being. Toki et al quoted Sayyid Qutb as portraying an "ideal interactive community as the one devoid of acrimonies; guided by Islamic precepts, and where solidarity reigns among the citizens for the

---

[24] See the Holy Qur'an 5:82.
[25] Op. Cit. Ibid. P. 106
[26] See the Most Holy Qur'an 3:64
[27] Al-Mubaligh quoted in Toki et'al P. 111
[28] See the Most Holy Qur'an 16:125
[29] See the Holy Bible 1st Thessalonians 5:21.

purpose of mutual security and peace"[30]. The Holy Qur'an stresses the unity of mankind in the following verse: "O mankind! Fear your Guardian Lord, who created you from a single person, created, out of it, his mate and from them twain scatted (like seeds) countless men and women; fear Allah, through Whom ye demand your mutual (right) be heedful of the wombs (that bore you); for Allah ever watches over you[31]. Kind treatment that fosters harmonious relationship among people of different socio-cultural backgrounds is further emphasized in the Qur'an thus: "Seest thou one who denies the judgment to come? Then such is the one who repulses the orphan. And encourages not the feeding of the indigent"[32] The verses do not specifically limit benevolent treatment to the Muslims only. As commanded by Allah, Muslims have been warned to shun aggression and should not condone aggression from any side. Islam maintains balance between war and peace.

What can be deciphered from the above in view of the prevailing realities in Nigeria is a radical departure from what the guiding principle and the sacred literatures of both Islam and Christianity stands for as it were. Hence the imperative of the philosophy of tolerance on both the ethnic and religious front as well as the necessity of an interfaith concept in its ideal sense that fully grapples with the existential situation of both Christians and Muslims for the enhancement of a stable, and peaceful relation amongst the diverse ethnic nationalities in Nigeria.

Enhancement of a Philosophy of Human Integration in Nigeria.

Several attempts have been made to argue for the place of interfaith dialogue as an enduring cultural philosophy which when adopted can lead to the enhancement of stable, secure and peaceful relations amongst the diverse ethnic nationalities in Nigeria. This argument is premised on the fact that role of religion in shaping the existential lives of any people and the fact that members of the diverse ethnic nationalities in Nigeria are adherents of one religion or the other.

---

[30] Toki et' al "Peace Building and Inter-Religious Dialogue in Nigeria" in *The Journal of Islam in Nigeria.* Vol. 1. No. 1, June, 2015. P. 111
[31] Chapter 4: 1 of the Most Holy Qur'an
[32] Ibid. chapter 107 verses 1 to 3

Interfaith concept properly situated stipulates an inter-religious dialogue. This dialogue is indispensible. This dialogue encourages people of different religious backgrounds to share knowledge of other people's religions on the platform of peace and unity. Inter-religious dialogue enhances knowledge of the differences and similarities between different religions and sects. The knowledge enriches the people how to crave for accommodation and mutual trust among themselves. Friendliness is better enhanced through dialogue. As such, violence and threat are eliminated[33].

It is quite imperative to state that "there is more to benefit in unity and to avoid the ricks of irrelevance and parochialism if only followers of religious traditions and cultural groups can reach out of their ghetto mentality of isolationism, exclusivism and denominationalism. More important, the idea that one's God is more God than the other's God cannot stand erect before any human court of reason"[34]. It is in this thinking that religion has been conceived under the prism of the paradox of "the one and the many"- one God with many ways of approaching and reaching to him. Hence, "no religion, whether Islam or Christianity, Hinduism or Buddhism can without a doctrine as to what is absolute and what is relative. Ditto the doctrinal language differs from one tradition to another. Nor can any religion be without a method of concentrating on the real and the living according to the it although the means again differs in different traditional climates…no religion is possible and man cannot attach himself to God without God having himself through his grace, provided the for doing so. Every orthodox religion is the choice of heaven and while still intact contains both the doctrines and methods which 'save' from his wretched terrestrial condition and opens to him the gates of heaven[35].

Deducible from the above is the fact that both Christianity and Islam share some basic elements in common and even where there exist some differences, the responses of Christians and Muslims should be the conceptions of each other's religion as "an alternative variants of the same phenomenon, to be assessed by a common criterion of their effectiveness in mediating

[33] Adukwu, R.M "Enhancing Christian/ Muslim Dialogue in Nigeria: Challenges for Reform Agenda" in *Religion and Sustainable Development* (ed) M.A Adesewo et al. A Publication of National Association for the Study of Religions and Education (Oyo: Haytee Press and Publisher, 2010). P. 390.
[34] Jim Unah quoted in Ihuah A.S. *Interrogating the God Question in Nigerian Politics: From the Dialogue of the Deaf to National Integration.* A Paper read at the Inauguration of the Benue State University Chapter of the Society for Peace Studies and Practice on Thursday, October 10th, 2013.
[35] Hossein Nasr *Ideas and Realities of Islam,* London: George Allen and Unwin, 1966) P. 15

between God and man"[36]. More importantly, adherents of Christianity and Islam shares the same humanity, and this should be the guiding principle behind any attempt at fostering an interfaith dialogue or relations. Our humanity as I have argued elsewhere is the gateway to the humanity of others and this lies in the uniqueness of ourselves and in accepting ourselves as the masterpiece of God. Our responsibility for others is the measure of our humanity; let us judge our own well being by the need of others, by uniting ourselves with them to a higher truth[37]. At this point, the dialogue of life becomes imperative.

The dialogue of life can help draw participants out of their cocoons of mutual mistrust and engender an atmosphere of deeper understanding, mutual esteem and respect. Beyond this, it is here argued that the dialogue of life offers us a more effective way of addressing issues of moral philosophy, which lies at the heart of the African sacred cosmos. When people that share the same economic, political, and cultural situation, such a basic dialogue is essential for the promotion of common human and spiritual values in the process of building a community of justice, solidarity, and peace. To be in this permanent dialogue is to be responding to the multiple voices from outside the circle of one's identity, voices calling one to cross over the boundaries and limitations of one's own experience and learn from others[38]. The approach in this dialogue (of life) should be that of love and a readiness for a deeper understanding of each other's point of view, and above all, by living out what we profess in our everyday life and leaving the issues as it were in the hands of God.

This is a form of dialogue of life that operates on practical and day-to-day terms. Christians and Muslims live next to each other; mingle freely in all aspects of human endeavor, meeting in the marketplace and on the streets, in schools and other institutions. Both Christians and Muslims are awakened every morning by the strident voice of the muezzin from the minaret of the mosque, urging faithful believers that "it is better to pray than to sleep." Christians receive Christmas and Easter greeting cards from their Muslim friends, neighbors, and relatives. Muslims are present in

---

[36] J.D.Y. Peel, "Engaging Islam in Nineteenth-Century Yorubaland," (NAMP Position Paper 27), P. 27
[37] See Ihuah A.S. *Interrogating the God Question in Nigerian Politics: From the Dialogue of the Deaf to National Integration.* A Paper read at the Inauguration of the Benue State University Chapter of the Society for Peace Studies and Practice on Thursday, October 10th, 2013.
[38] Akintunde E. Akinade The Precarious Agenda: Christian-Muslim Relations in Contemporary Nigeria *being a lecture delivered in Professor Jane Smiths' "Essentials of Christian-Muslim Relations" class in the summer of 2002.* P. 3.

churches for the baptism, wedding, or burial of relatives and friends. In this dialogue of life, Christians and Muslims are enriched by each other's experience and spirituality and strengthened by certain features of the faith of the other[39]. While we yet grapple with the reality of the existence of conflict in human life and in Nigeria in particular in view of the heterogeneous nature of our existential condition, since the battles on the barricades are ultimately rooted in conflict of the mind, let us be ever prepared, while an issue remains unresolved even after we have exhausted our last agreement, to begin again, at this time in our history, more than ever before, if necessary, informed and frank discussions in the line of the dialogue of life and eschew as it were, the dialogue of the deaf.

In this thinking, "the domination of, and discrediting other religions different from one's own religion is itself irreligious, and mischievous. There must be a disposition to discuss values in the assumption that nobody has a monopoly of truth and that everyone has some share in it. Above all, there must be a preparedness to endorse publicly the values at the heart of all religious traditions and ethnic grouping. There must be a search for values which are in need of particular nuance to cope with life today"[40]. It is only at the point that the interfaith concept will find relevance both as an enduring thought pattern as well as a philosophy built on tolerance that possesses the tendency of driving a programme of action in enhancing a stable, secured and peaceful relation amongst the diverse ethnic entities in Nigeria.

Conclusion

As I draw to the conclusion of this presentation, there are a few issues I want to rehearse and they include, first, Nigeria is a multi-ethnic, multi-lingual and multi-religious nation. This fact should be harnessed in the positive direction and not in   the other way round. Hence, those things that serve to unite us should be elevated over and against those indices that divides us. Secondly, this paper has observed and makes bold to stipulate that the failure of the Nigerian state as it were, constitutes one of the major reasons why this violent conflicts and mistrust have ensured and thrived amongst the diverse ethnic groups in Nigeria. This failure can be argued in two fronts: the first being the inability of the leadership of the nation state as it were to provide her citizen with a level playing ground, the goods of human flourishing and employment

---

[39] Ibid.
[40] Op. Cit Ihuah, P. 14

15

opportunities. The absence of which has led to the availability of unemployed youths in their numbers to be used as the dramatist personnel in crisis and conflict situations be it ethnic or religious; the second, closely linked with the first has to do with corruption which entails the appropriation to oneself, resources meant to alleviate the collective sufferings of the people. This undoubtedly leads to the continual widening of the gap between the rich and the poor, the haves and the have-not and hence, the absence of social justice and the propensity of revolt and violent crisis or conflicts.

While it is accepted as true, the fact that the fight against corruption by the President Mohammadu Buhari led administration is not yielding positive results on a daily basis. This brings to the fore, the imperativeness of a collective effort to strengthen the institutions saddled with the responsibility of redirecting the Nigerian ship of national reconstruction of the Nigerian state for the better.

It must also be stated here that the prevalence of violent conflicts that have been instigated by ethnic and religious jingoists cannot be said to be a blessing to our collective existence. In fact, these crises have only served to further push back the frontiers of development and have demonstrated themselves as constituting clogs in the wheel of the progress of the Nigerian state. It is not however clear whether the Nigerian leadership is not part of the problem of national cohesion. In a recent interview with Nigerian President on CNN, Amanpour, a journalist of repute, reveals the complicity of the Nigerian leadership in the hostilities of the herdsmen against virtually all the tribe in Nigeria. In her words,

> By all definitions and descriptions, the Nigeria's so called herdsmen are terrorists and if President Buhari doesn't believe so, then it would be difficult for anyone to reasonably absolve him (Buhari) from complicity. I cover wars and crisis as a journalist, I think I know, and the world also knows how terrorists operate. The fact that herdsmen's attacking pattern is focused primarily on wiping off farmers should rob Buhari who has achieved only little in his economic agenda that's expected to be powered mainly by farmers. The impact of these well-defined attacks on Nigeria's economy are expected to be grave, maybe on the long run

greater than that of Boko Haram which has been largely localized to the North East".[41]

That Christians, Muslims and the traditionalist religious institution (atheists inclusive) have a common origin from one God is not in doubt. What this means is that we possess and share the same humanity and hence, our attitudes and response to all religious traditions should be that of the dialogue of life hinged on the thinking that that all religious traditions are alternative variants of the same phenomenon. This thinking will no doubt push back the frontiers of the "holier than thou" attitude and elevating one's God as better than the other person's God as well as profiling one's ethnic group as superior to the other. It is on the basis of this dialogue of life as against the dialogue of the deaf that a stable, secured and peaceful coexistence can be established between the over 250 ethnic nationalities in Nigeria.

---

[41] Christiane Amanpour, CNN, https://www.acnntv.com/herdsmen-are-terrorists-and-buhari-may-be-behind-them-cnn-reporter/ (accessed on Friday 24th May, 2019)